How to Create Kenpo Karate

BOOK TWO

The Secret of Forms

Al Case

Quality Press

Copyright © 2014 by Alton H. Case

For more information go to:

MonsterMartialArts.com

Table of Contents

Introduction   5

Matrix Kenpo Forms   7

Short One   8

Conclusion to the Forms   17

Advanced Forms   18

Analysis of Purple Techniques   20

Blue Belt Techniques   67

About the Author   123

introduction

How to Create Kenpo Karate consists of three volumes.

The first volume has the history, including the mistakes of the pioneers, and the analysis of 54 kenpo techniques.

The second volume continues with the analysis of techniques, and includes a short section on how to revise and recreate the forms of Kenpo.

The third volume concludes the analysis of techniques, then presents a complete revision of Kenpo, including all belts, and the matrixing theory behind this. You will learn how to write a matrix of your own at this point, though for complete information on how to make and use matrixes you are recommended to view the series called 'Matrixing Karate.'

HOW TO MATRIX KENPO FORMS

Kenpo forms need to be reworked to fit the Matrix Kenpo that you are learning.

Forms are not just a sequence of techniques, they are a way to practice without a partner, a way to insert the basic/basics into your art, such as relaxing, breathing, grounding, alignment and loose-tight.

Now, I am going to give you the first form, and explain certain things, and then I am going to give you some advice that will help you create the forms for your matrix Kenpo.

Yes...YOUR Matrix Kenpo.

You are not going to agree with everything I say, you are going to shuffle the order of the techniques, tweak and alter, and come up with something that you feel is better than what I have presented here.

And, let's be honest, it might be better.

This is an art, and art is dependent upon imagination, so which of you has more imagination than me?

I'm pretty up there with logic, but...imagine, if you will, and see what kind of limits you can throw off.

Okay, here is the first form, it is called Short One.

SHORT ONE

Stand naturally.

Step back with the left foot into a deep horse stance as you execute a right inward block. A deeper stance makes your legs work harder, and your tan tien, and thus you create more energy.

Pivot into a bow stance as you execute a left punch. Snap the hips to put more body weight into the strike.

Step back with the right foot into a deep horse stance as you execute a left inward block. Make sure you breath in when you contract, and out when you expand.

Pivot into a bow stance as you execute a right punch. Have somebody push on your fist to make sure the body alignment to the ground is correct.

Step forward with the right foot and turn into a deep horse stance to the left as you execute a left outward block. Make sure you relax between movements.

Pivot into a bow stance as you execute a right punch. Feel the weight go down the front leg, and up into the tan tien.

Step back with the left leg into a deep horse stance as you execute a right outward block. Move all the body parts at the same time.

Pivot into a bow stance as you execute a left punch. Breath out when you strike something, or block, or get struck or blocked.

Move the front foot across your body and turn to face 180 degrees in the other direction. synchronize breathing and body motion.

Pivot into a bow stance as you execute a right punch. Practice relaxing before the strike, this is 'loose-tight,' this is focusing your energy.

Step back with the left leg into a deep horse stance as you execute a right high block. Look your opponent in the eyes, you can't fight what you can't face.

Pivot into a bow stance as you execute a left punch. Grip the ground with your feet, feel your weight sink into the earth.

Step forward with the left foot and face to the right in a deep horse stance as you execute a right low block. A tight fist is a heavy fist, but you must relax before you tighten.

Pivot into a bow stance as you execute a left punch. It's not how hard you hit, it's how much weight you can put into the strike.

Step back with the right leg into a deep horse stance as you execute a left low block. Make the world silent around you, that is the secret of creating energy.

Pivot into a bow stance as you execute a right punch. Do this form a thousand times; do the art until the art does you.

Return to the natural stance. The highest art is not to beat up an enemy, it is to make an enemy into a friend.

Conclusion to the Forms

Okay, you may have noticed that this form is like the original short one. But, there are a few things you need to know.

One, you can teach this with just the blocks. Maybe for a yellow belt, if you still have one.

Two, the stances are lower. This creates more energy, or power. Simply, if you bend lower, your legs work harder, and your tan tien has to create more energy, and this energy will go directly into your body and art.

Three, you must practice it with each of the basic/basics, focusing on each in turn, until the basic/basics are part of you. That means do it once with relaxing, do it once with breathing, do it once with grounding, do it once with proper body alignment (have somebody push gently on your form to check it), do it once with loose-tight. Then do this sequence again. And again and again until you become a powerful machine. A powerful Kenpo machine.

Look, get truthful Look at the way people do Kenpo, and you will see they are high in their stances. Lazy, if you will. So get lower, start putting energy into your body.

Four, you can have another form by adding a simultaneous block to the punch.

Five, Parker was powerful because he had Okinawan Karate as a base. But, as time went on he changed his system, and he neglected the base. Okay, put it back in, and without having to learn Okinawan Karate, just do the basic/basics in your form.

Now, the preceding all stated, and a structure of three potential forms described so that you may power up your art right from the get go, let's discuss the forms past Short One.

ADVANCED FORMS

I have an interesting little trick that I use, it is called geometry.

I do forms on a square. Then I do them on a foursquare. Then I do them on a nine square.

This does not negate classical footwork, it only makes it better.

Believe me, when you do the logic of matrixing your classical ALWAYS gets better. And the reason for this is because you understand the moves and motions underlying the more advanced moves.

So take a nine square, take the first few techniques, and do them, moving from square to square. Here's what it looks like.

9	10	11
2 8	1 7 13	6 12
3	4	5

Draw a nine square pattern on the ground. Move from square to square, following the numbers, doing techniques.

You can do one technique and drill it.

You can alternate two techniques, or three, and learn how to put these things together.

You can pick out 12 techniques, and step back into the 13th square to end the form.

You can do all 20 techniques, one after the other, learning how to fit one motion into another.

And, eventually, you will come up with a preferred sequence of techniques.

Some won't work together, others will be a dream, but let me tell you something, and this applies to all the techniques, everything we've done, and everything in your whole durned life:

You learn more from making mistakes than from succeeding.

Yes, succeeding feels better.

But failing teaches you something.

It shows you how to fix things.

It enables you to come to grips with your mistakes, maybe even your faults.

So go through each belt level, alter the geometry you do on the nine square, find different patterns, learn how to make mistakes, and how to grow bigger because of them.

technique 55
Broken Honor A

Defense for Shaking Hands.

A perfectly good technique, ruined by the fact of attacking somebody during an act of friendship. Whoever mae this one up is twisted.

Step forward between legs with left foot.

Swing arm up (helping with the other hand) and turn to break the elbow over the shoulder.

Now, if this was done with an attacker grabbing the wrist, it would be great. the only problem is that you are mixing kicks, which is long distance, with grab arts, which are close distance. Fine, put it at a higher ranking than purple.

Step around with back leg to force attacker to circle.

Wheel kick to plexus with ball of foot, or the stomach with the instep.

Cross out.

It is a good technique, but there are too many parts for a beginner.

technique 56
Descending Arrow C

Defense for two handed choke from rear.

This is one of those iconic kenpo techniques. Everybody recognizes it as Kenpo. Here's the problem...too much work with one hand. Why not just use the other hand to punch? Maybe punch low, then do your elbow strike up.

Step to one side in front of own foot, pivot and swing arm to break hold.

Bring swinging arm through, then reverse to upward elbow strike to face.

Bring arm down with back knuckle to face.

Claw face.

This is a good technique, but I would change it slightly, according to the recommendations stated earlier.

technique 57
Descending Arrow D

Defense for two handed choke from rear, but previous technique (Descending Arrow C) fails to break hold.

I like this. It is the first time Kenpo recognizes that things might not go as planned. It is what we call, in Matrixing, going through a door. Simply, you must be prepared to go through three or four doors, through or four 'what ifs,' if you are going to really be adequate in your martial arts.

 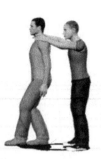

Pivot back from the failed break and execute hammerfist to groin.

Step to one side in front of own foot, pivot and swing arm to break hold.

Yes. Leave it in.

technique 58
Descending Arrow E

Defense for two handed choke from rear.

The problem here is that the defender should combine breaking the hold with an elbow strike to the face. No need for a second technique, but, if there is, the attacker is now facing, and the defender is backing up. Mind you, i have nothing wrong with the final two elbow strikes as they are shown here, but they are a little busy for one arm, and there is the missed opportunity of the earlier elbow strike.

Pivot back from the failed break and execute hammerfist to groin.

Step out and across.
Pivot and break hold with swinging arm.

Elbow strike to face with swing arm.
Elbow spike to face with same arm.

technique 59
Twisted Wing D

Defense for armlock.

This is a good technique. The reason it gets away with being a little busy is that you go from an elbow to a lock, and you stick with the knees and elbows for the later defense. And, in this situation, the lock works.

Step forward with armlock side, other side elbow to face.

Circle the arm to lock the elbow.

Step and pivot and swing attacker around.
Knee to mid-section.

Hammerfist to neck.

technique 60
Twisted Wing E

Defense for armlock.

On the other hand, I don't like this one. The break is weak, hitting somebody in the groin after you break their arm is...odd. Breaking the arm in this position doesn't seem likely. And so on.

Step forward elbow to arm (break).

Hammerfist to groin.

The above stated, I admit that my notes on this one were lacking. Had to go looking for other people's versions. And, in addition, I seemed to have my techniques out of order. So include that in your estimation before you totally discard this technique.

technique 61
Hidden Key A

Defense for two handed lapel grab.

Interesting technique. Good lock and punch. You could go over or under, work the radials, and so on, and it works.

And, a scoop kick works.

And, a chop REALLY works.

But a scoop and a chop together don't work.

Lock grip.

Middle knuckle to plexus while stepping forward.

Scoop kick to groin while chopping to neck with lock hand, and step back.

Knife edge kick to far knee.

So make a couple of techniques out of it.

But doing two things of this nature splits the energy in the body, and splits the intention of the defender.

Oh, and you already know that a knife edge kick is not a weight bearing, and thus delivering, kick.

I opt, in the case of the knife edge kick, to use it like a 'slapper,' slapping the side of the foot, like a reverse crescent kick, against the knee. This would work, and work well.

I often wonder if a lower level reverse crescent kick was actually what was in the mind of the people who thought this stuff up, and then it got weird when it went from teacher to teacher, from culture to culture.

Maybe, if we look at the types of clothes worn a couple of hundred years ago, we might figure it out.

technique 62
Lifting the Chopsticks A

Defense against overhead club attack.

A classic and good technique. The only problem was with my artwork.
I put the elbow in the armpit instead of the temple. That's okay, it will work
there, too. But the temple is better.

Step forward with same side leg and execute a crossed wrist block.
Execute an elbow roll

Elbow to temple.
Elbow to spine.
Cross out, or takedown?

technique 63
Key to the Sword

Defense for shoulder grab from the side.

A good technique, but you have to make sure your lock is really tight. The thing is, this is one of those kenpo techniques that live up to Kenpo. You can pull the guy off balance, and the strikes work, and you can actually get away with having one side too busy.

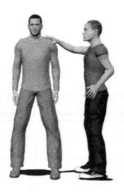 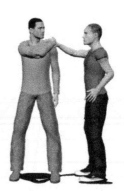

Lock grab hand with cross hand.

Step back into horse and execute a middle knuckle to the attacker's upper arm.

Strike middle knuckle to the armpit.

Circle arm and bring down on forearm (breaking).
Chop neck.
Cross out.

technique 64
Snapping the Limb

Defense for a right punch.

My bad notes. You can see the defender's foot is on the outside, and then it is on the inside. My oops. So start on the inside and it will work better with no mystical moves.

Step back and guide punch past and hook.
Break elbow with palm thrust.

The problem here is that there are several ways to hook, and a good hook should set up the break, and it might work. Might.

Back knuckle to face.
Elbow strike to face.

Groin grab.

Rip groin up and elbow jaw.

In spite of my bad notes, the technique still isn't doing it for me. It turns into a typical kenpo 'busy hand.' Too busy to be effective as a real technique.

So change this for a better trap and break, be willing to roll it into an armbar or elbow roll, then takedown. That is the better way to do this technique, and it will hold to the rule of which weapon to use when collapsing distance.

technique 65
Sting of the Bee

Defense against a left punch.

Step to a cat stance and circle the front hand outward.
Shuffle forward and snap fingers to eyes.

The kenpo spearhand is a weird thing. You stiffen two fingers and bend the middle finger, and that works weird things on intention and the transmission of energy. Guaranteed, the stiff fingers, all fingers, spear hand is the best. I say this after near 50 years of playing with the thing.

That said, this is a great technique, very bread and butter, nothing like a poke to the eyes to end a fight.

But, I wonder why there was nothing else on the technique? What happened to all the busy work and follow ups and everything? The one technique which needs it doesn't have it.

So try adding a kick to the groin.

I mean, why not?

I always tell students that they can use the spear hand when they can do push ups on it. This is good advice, and I recommend it to you and all your students.

technique 66
Ox Cart A

Defense for two hand choke from rear.

Not a good technique.

First, there is the assumption that the fellow is going to just grab with long arms and stand there.

Second, the grabs are difficult, the motion is difficult, and the whole thing of step and turn while somebody has you, in this specific technique, is...odd.

This is one of those techniques I think they gave to children to keep them out of the way while the men played.

Reach up and overhead and grip wrists.

Step to side and turn, twining the arms and breaking them against each other.

Snap kick to groin.

Hammerfist to groin.

Now, the above stated, there is a piece of gold in this technique: the arm twine.

But you don't normally break with an arm twine, unless you are lacking. You throw. Throwing is more difficult, requires more control, and is therefore better art.

Yes, the kick will work, and it is good if the twine doesn't work.

A much better entry is a lapel grab with a punch. Slap the punch over the holding arm, twine, and throw.

I have come across other versions of this, one has a nice elbow spike to the plexus, which, on retrospect, turns a little silly unless the technique doesn't work. I mean, why go out from a throw, unless you need a shock and lock because it messed up? And, I hate to say it, but I may have messed certain things up with my graphics. This was a hard one to visualize and the software fought me, didn't want to do certain things with the human body.

technique 67
Flapping Wing C

Defense for two hand grab to lapel.

Not a bad technique. A little busy, but tidy nonetheless.

Lock with right hand.

Step back with right foot.
Eye jab with left hand.
Rake forearms down.

Chop to throat.
Cross out.

technique 68
Flapping Wing D

Defense for two hand grab to lapel.

Not as tidy as the last one. I'm not a big fan of back fists. They look good, but they don't move the bag. They are more of an irritant or a distraction than a good fighting technique.

After the back knuckles we are into the last technique. I would just stick with the last one and toss this one.

Lock hands.
Step back.
Start figure eight with fore knuckles slash to head.

End figure eight with back knuckles to head.

Rake forearms.

Chop throat.

One thing to think about, this is the place to do an armbar. Armbar and spike or such. It would be a better technique.

technique 69
The Shield

Right punch to face.

Surprisingly, I don't have much problem with the high block circling all the way around. I used to do a technique like that in classical karate, and it REALLY worked. So, good.

You may want to step forward and to the left side a bit more. That's probably the way it was done.

Step forward with left leg and parry with the left hand.
Right upward block knocking attacker's arm up.

Swing upward block all the way around to reverse hammerfist to groin.
Claw face with left hand.

I do have a problem with the claw to the face. It doesn't fit the flow of body, and it also creates busy work.

Shuffle forward and execute a right elbow to the body.

technique 70
Sacred Sacrifice

Blocking a right kick from kneeling position.
Not bad. A little odd, but not bad.

Pivot the body to the left as you execute a right palm block downward.

Right hammerfist to groin.
Back knuckle to plexus.

The problems start with the back knuckles to the solar plexus. It's a weak weapon to a target of mass. The hammerfist to the gorin is weak enough.

Yes, I know you can snap those suckers, and that can do the trick.

There are easier things to do, like punching the knee sideways (lots of points there!) and collapsing the attacker.

Drop to hands and execute a rear kick with the right leg.

But for a weird situation, it's not a bad defense. Makes you think.

technique 71
Descending Arrow E

Escape from two handed choke from the rear.

I've seen this technique done with a single shoulder grab from rear, and it makes slightly more sense.

But the whole technique isn't bad, except for the fact that after you strike a fellow once, he is going to move, be moved out of position, and so on.

So this technique is a poser part of the time. Still, it is excellent for drilling beginners on different and multiple strikes.

Cross step to side, while swinging arm over and down.

Punch.

 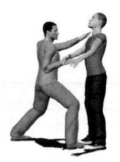

Half fist punch.
Spearhand.

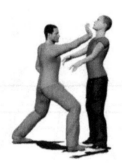

Palm thrust.

The best way to do this technique, however, is with an elbow strike. Catching and pulling on the turn, then uncorking an elbow strike, and so on.

technique 72
Lifting the Chopsticks B

Defense against right overhead club attack.

Nice technique. I disagree with breaking over throwing or locking, but that is philosophical, and everybody has a different philosophy. the main thing is...does it work? And, yes. Works good.

Step forward with the left foot as you execute an upper crossed wrist block.

Arm bar break at chest level.

Right wheel kick to plexus.

The wheel kick can be with the instep, but kicking with the ball of the foot puts more weight into a smaller impact area, and because it requires better control is more artistic.

technique 73
Fluttering Leaves

Defense for two handed throat grab from front.

A good one. Mind you, the hands are busy, but they are alternating, and speed can be built up, so it is classic Kenpo.

I would prefer an attack instead of simply breaking the grab on the first move. After all, if he is holding you, he is holding himself.

But why be picky. Good stuff.

Step back as you execute a double outward block with knife hands.

Right chop to ribs.
Left chop to throat.

Right spear to solar plexus.
Left chop to groin.
Cross out.

technique 74
Slaying the Dragon

Defense against a right punch.

Snap and pull is good, but if you have pulled him over it is hard to wheel a knee strike to the plexus. You can see that I kneed a little higher, and that because the fellow is still bent over. Well, heck. You just slammed his kidney and neck, he's probably going to go down rather than up.

To tell the truth, this works better if you pull him into the wheeling knee, then hammer him.

Circle both arms clockwise, right hand palm block and left hand loose. Left hand palm snap to break elbow.

Continue pulling opponent over, and execute simultaneous hammers to spine and back of neck.

Wheel knee strike to solar plexus.
You know, it is not a bad technique, just needs some tweaking.

One other tweak, aside from the knee first, is to use the hammers one after the other, not simultaneous. I am not a fan of double strikes, or double blocks, except in rare cases. I just don't like splitting intention down two sides of the body, I don't like splitting my energy.

The wheeling knee is not commonly seen, but it is a very good technique. I couldn't believe it when it worked in freestyle. The thing is...nobody has seen it, so if you practice it diligently it might just become a very useful part of your arsenal.

technique 75
Burning Cinders

Defense for two hands on throat (or lapel) from front.

Okay, we were doing so good, and then this technique comes along.

Lock and knuckle are okay, though I would prefer a power punch to the plexus. But...okay.

Lock hands with left hand.

Right hand middle knuckle to plexus.
Pull arms apart.

It is not that easy to separate the arms of somebody who is grabbing onto you like this. If they are so enraged that they will put their hands on you, then chances are they are powering up. Believe me, I've tried, and hands don't just fly apart, even if softened up by a middle knuckle to the plexus.

Right elbow to head.
Left hand grabs chin.

Break neck.
Right chop to throat.

But here's the real problem...do you think that guy is just going to stand there and let you break his neck? Even if you have shocked him with a GREAT elbow strike, what is the first thing people do when you lay hands on them as in a grab? They tighten up, they get ready to wrestle, and even if you did a GREAT elbow strike and they are half out on their feet...they would clinch! It's instinctive! People clinch when they get clocked. Watch any boxing match if you don't believe.

And, not to beat on this point, but it takes power and weight and leverage to break a neck in this fashion. Yes, if you have a top mount position of some kind, but that means you are wrestling, or doing MMA, or some other sort of thing!

In spite of the adequate beginning, there are a LOT better techniques than this one.

technique 76
Lightening Flash A

Defense against right upward knife thrust to belly.

This isn't a bad technique. It's not the best, but it is kenpo, and it isn't bad. What's nice is that this technique, and the next two (variations b and c), allow for much practice. It's sort of intuitive, which makes it nice for a beginner.

Step forward and to the left.
Left palm block to the elbow.
Right hand chops the attacker's wrist.

Right hand claws the eyes.

technique 77
Lightening Flash B

Defense against right upward knife thrust to belly.

Step forward and to the left.
Left palm block to the elbow.
Right hand chops the attacker's wrist.

Right hand spears the eyes.

technique 78
Lightening Flash C
Defense against right upward knife thrust to belly.

Step forward and to the left.
Left palm block to the elbow.
Right hand chops the attacker's wrist.

Right hand four finger (split spear) strike to eyes.

I've turned the split spear sideways so you can see it better. Obviously, it would be straightened so as to poke both eyes.

Now, I think this is the only weakness of the technique.

Most people, no matter how long they practice, are going to be able to do a split finger spear, and I question the workability even if they did. There is the split of energy and intention when you use your hand this way,.

technique 79
Hidden Key B

Defense against two handed lapel grab.

Good technique. I would use a power punch on the key strike to the plexus, but, hey, that's personal preferences at this point.

The thing is, this is right up the center, going to make the attacker hurt and flinch. Or is that flinch and hurt?

Lock with left hand.

Step forward and strike plexus with middle knuckle
Bring right elbow up through arms (breaking grip) to elbow the face.

Right claw to face
Cross out.

technique 80
Flapping Wing E

Defense against two handed lapel grab.

Good technique, but should be done with one hand, or maybe just a punch. Also, the upward elbow break isn't highly efficient. Better to use a dangling forearm with a spin. The whole body can get behind the spin.

Lock hands with left hand.

Step back with left leg into horse.
Strike elbows from below with right forearm.
Right middle knuckle to solar plexus.

Cross step with the left foot.
Spin to horse with elbow strike.
I would just tweak this one a bit.

technique 81
Clinging Vines

Defense for two men grabbing wrists from each side with one hand each.

I always thought this wouldn't work, but actually had occasion to use it one night. Absolutely devastating...since I didn't use the knife edges. I used a side thrust kick on the first guy, blew him across the room, and the second guy let go and wanted to be somewhere else desperately.

That said, tweak it for power kicks, and teach it to slightly more advanced people. It didn't work for me until I was a first brown.

Cross step behind pulling one opponent off balance.

Knife edge to mid section of the off balance attacker.
Knife edge foot cross steps to the front.

Rear leg scoop kick to leg.

Same foot knife edge to the attacker's far knee.

Cross out.

Blue Belt Techniques

technique 82
Thousand Mallets

Defense against a right punch.

This is one that I remember to this day, it just seemed so cool and logical. The problem is that my instructions said strike the mid-section, but in variationsI have seen, the instructions are to strike the groin (as I have shown), which makes me think that other people have seen the problem here.

If you strike somebody in the mid-section they might fold, and they might not. If they fold, the thing works, but if they don't, you just have a mess.

I know Parker was trying to train beginners, and the idea is to have the attacker move accordingly, but there is sometimes a major disconnect. I have hit people in the belly...HARD, and they have grinned. So, in spite of the coolness of this technique, I would have the mid-section strike, which is good, but then I wouldn't rely on the attacker folding so politely. Major tweaking to make this work. A whole reworking to account for the fact that people don't always bend over. And I don't think a few variations, in the even the does or doesn't bend, would work. False expectations, you know?

Step forward with the left foot with an inward block, right arm down and slightly back.

Pivot left and strike mid-section with left forearm as you cock the left arm high.

Pivot other way with left hammer to kidney and cocking right arm up.
Right hammer to neck.

Pull left leg behind right leg to cat stance as you right back knuckle the
temple.

Right claw to face.

Cross out.

technique 83
Parting the Beads

Defense against two handed push to chest.

Excellent technique. Should be done earlier, and then a part B with some sort of follow up. Maybe an elbow smash to the head followed by an elbow spike to the face.

Step back into cat stance as you circle the arms out and execute a double parry.

Snap kick to groin.

technique 84
Releasing the Eagle

Defense against hand on shoulder.

The key strike is interesting here. I am not opposed to it, except that I wonder if somebody is going to wait for the second key strike. Maybe. Depends on the speed of the defense.

And, I like spinning the guy around.

But the reverse chop is awkward. The locking hand is suddenly out of place, should change into a parry or something. And I'm not sure if my notes meant a chop with the rear foot hand, or a ridge hand.

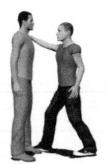 

Lock and step away as you execute a key strike to the upper arm.

Key strike to the armpit.
Circle the arm to bend the attacker's arm.

Cross step and pivot to force attacker around.
Reverse chop to the throat.

Interestingly enough, I have seen later versions working a hip throw. I think this opens the door, but I don't think a hip throw is the solution.

Why not force the attacker down by pressing down on the arm?

Why not punch instead of chop?

Mind you, I don't think the technique is necessarily weak, just needs to be tweaked a bit.

technique 85
Tumbling Samurai

Defense for push from behind.

Look, this should not be a technique...it should be a training drill at the beginning of class. Maybe with the 'technique' that deals with breakfalls.'

Shoulder roll to a horse facing the attacker.

Chicken kick.

Chicken kick? Better to do a front kick, or side thrust, but not a knife edge side kick as some would have you do.

The point here is that if you leap into the air and fly at somebody, back in the sixties people would panic. Never been seen before.

And, I actually saw it used in a real street fight a couple of years ago. Kid pulled it off, knocked the bully down (who was bigger), and then beat feet for safety.

Cross out.

So, it works, but it is better practiced with different kicks, but would be better as a way to open a semi-advanced class.

Not beginners. They are having trouble rolling, or doing a flying kick. But once they have a modicum of experience, it actually isn't bad.

technique 86
Escape of the Lamb B

Defense for choke from rear.

Now, the hands get in the way, I haven't lowered the head for the spin under the grab, my software had a lot of trouble doing this one, and I might have even screwed up the stepping and pivoting.

But, it is workable. In classical karate there is a crescent kick that we use to block a punch. It is in the third form Pinan Three (Heian Three), and it really works. You can block a punch with a foot easily.

But, as I said, the hands get in the way of this technique, and it seems a little busy, but my main thing is this: you are going from a grab art attack, which calls for knees and elbows, to a kick MUCH better suited to a certain distance.

Cross step with chop to groin.

Pivot and ridge hand to groin.
Cross step.

Pivot.

Crescent kick to head.
Cross out.

One question, if you hit a guy in the groin he is going to probably cover up pretty quick, which makes the second strike to the groin not really worthwhile. Still, it is interesting, and maybe...?

My complaints noted, I sort of like the technique, just for people who are advanced. Kicking that close, you have to be advanced to make it work.

technique 87
Lobster's Claws B

Defense for two hand grab to wrists from the front.

Nice, simple escape, teaches a beginner to sink his weight into the ground, should be done sooner in the student's training.

Step forward and side to horse, snapping the arms straight down to break through the thumbs.

Circle the hands inward to double back knuckle to head.

technique 88
Chinese Eclipse

Defense against a right punch.

Yikes! Start with a beginner's technique, which is good, but doesn't set up for follow ups, then add a string of follow ups that expect the opponent to just stand there.

It would be easy to make this a simple technique and end with the first punch, but difficult to make it an advanced technique or variation.

Step forward and to the left into a horse stance with a left Inward block. Right punch to mid-section.

Left reverse back knuckle (corkscrew punch) to rear of head. Shuffle with right spear (inverted? palm up?) to floating rib.

Left claw to eyes.
Shuffle with right elbow to floating rib.
Cross out.

Further, I have to say that I don't recommend anybody do spear hands unless they can do push ups on the spear.

technique 89
Lobster's Claws C

Defense against two hands grabbing wrists in front.

Pretty good. I don't think I would pose the hands though. Just rake down the forearms, getting more forward head bob, then continue with the backfist and etc.

Punch downward as you step forward into horse.

Step forward and circle both hands outward on one side to force arms down. One hand over the other.

Backfist to face.
Punch to solar plexus.

technique 89
Crumbling Statue A

Defense for right punch.

Great technique up until the heel thrust. The technique is too busy then. A student's time would be best served by learning to control while on the ground.

I mean, stomp the kidneys, quad the spine, then knuckle the head into concrete...can we have a little mercy here? Or maybe just a little control?

And, to tell the truth, you can flip a guy without the palm strikes. Just slide in and grab the neck and do it.

Step left to horse with left hand parry then right hand outward block.

Shuffle as you circle hands to double Palm Thrust to kidneys.

There is an art to violence, but the true art is in control.
Maybe just a heel stomp, then cover out.

Grab shoulders and pivot to bow, pulling attacker over the stance to land on his front.

Right heel thrust to kidney.

Right knee on back.
Right punch to the head.

technique 90
Whirlpool

Defense against a right punch.

A good technique, but it gets a little bit...weird.

Good block and neck break, and the sword hand is good if you can get it through. Remember, you just blocked his arm into the way.

But, if you get it, good hold. Quick and easy. Break or sleep. Tap, snap, or nap. BUT...why do you have to punch a guy after you break his neck?

And, again, why not practice a little control on the ground?

Step left to horse with left inward block.
Right hand reverse sword to throat.

Right foot circles in back of attacker, left hand behind head to grasp right sword hand.

Pull to break neck.

Left foot steps back with the left hand pulling hair.
Pull to the kneeling position.
Right punch to the face.

technique 91
Silkscreen A

Defense against right hand shoulder grab with left hand punch.

The weakness in this technique is going under the grab arm to block. Heck, go under, and you've just passed the first arm, which means you missed one block already!

Also, I had trouble understanding my notes here, and it looks like the counter grab to the elbow is awkward.

So the solution would be to block the grab arm, catching the wrist of the grab arm with your right hand, then shifting the grip so you can do an armbar pull. This isn't the greatest solution, but it's adequate. But it does lead into knees to the face and that sort of thing.

Or, maybe block the punch and twine the arms. I really like that one, and the counter grab opens to the door to complete flips.

Yes, wait for the punch and block it across the grab arm. You'll have to work to catch the grab arm, but I still think it is easier than the original.

Right hand cross lock hand.

Left inward block and left kick to groin.
Left hand grab the grab hand above the elbow.

Step back to horse while pulling elbow.
Right palm thrust to chin.
Cross out.

I love a good palm thrust to the chin.

The fact of the matter is that this technique does open a lot of doors, many of them complex, and there are going to be a lot of opinions and variations on how to solve this less than adequate but brilliant technique.

technique 92
Ox Cart B

Defense against two hand choke from rear.

I have to say, I am not really a fan of this grab his wrists, turn and twist. The pieces are brilliant, I love the twine, but they don't fit together.

I would teach the twine from a push, pass one hand over the other, and twine that sucker into a takedown or, advanced, a throw (with a shoulder roll out).

Grab wrists.

Step to the right.
Cross step and turn, twining the arms.

Break arms with knee.
Same foot snap kick to the groin.

I also have trouble with the break of arms with a knee, then the kick. That leg is getting too busy. Break and throw, or kick and elbow, but not everything but the kitchen sink all at once and all together.

Step forward and elbow strike to the face.
So a push to a twine, a kick and an elbow.
Or, variation, twine to knee break, then elbow.

technique 93
Hand of the Dragon B

Defense for one hand choke from front.

This technique is better with a kick (variation A) or a throw. It gets a little too tight when you are doing this kind of wrist lock with an elbow.

Grab with same side hand and peel choking hand.

As he falls knee him in the ribs.

Punch to the face.

I would leave this out, or tighten up the wrist lock, make sure it doesn't go into an armbar, and work on taking the guy down.

By this time in a martial artist's career he should be obsessing on control, not just looking for new and better ways to damage.

technique 94
Hand of the Dragon C

Defense for one hand choke from front.

Good technique. Explores control. Jumps into grab art extrapolations.

Grab with same side hand and peel choking hand.

Wrap own arm around their neck.

Punch the base of the skull.

Might need an elbow for this strike to the skull, saves the hands, allows more body twist, excellent for looking at weapons you use when the distance collapses.

Would make a variation, just explore it a bit, have them do the elbow, and save the fist for alternative solutions.

technique 95
Hand of the Dragon D

Defense for one hand choke from front.

Takedown and control. Not break. We're just getting carried away with destruction, when the true art is in control.

Grab with same side hand and peel choking hand.

Pull up as you stomp the ribs.

Counter grab the attacker's wrist.

Pivot to kneeling stance and break attacker's arm on your knee.

Cross out.

technique 96
Driving the Spike

Defense for punch.

What a dilemma! The quintessential Kenpo technique. Builds speed, builds the kenpo mystique, but...one hand is too busy, and the dummy has to wait for the technique, and then he has to respond as prescribed, and not as a real person would react.

To tell the truth, I would make this an exercise, maybe done at the beginning of class, or before techniques, to warm a person up and get him going in the kenpo frame of mind. It's more of a drill than a technique, anyway.

Step right with an inward block.
Step back slightly as you chop the throat.

Shuffle in with an elbow to face.
Hammerfist to groin.

Back knuckle to face.
Palm thrust.
Cross out.

technique 97
Crossing Swords A

Defense for a right punch.

This is pretty good. Solid block, I'd prefer a kick with the front leg, it's closer, but that's okay, you'd twist up the right and left aspects if you did.

The only problem is the web of the thumb and forefinger to the throat. You hit, then you have to go back and under the arm. Better to lift the arm sooner and do an elbow to the chest, glancing strike on the way to the arm break, but it's not a bad technique.

Right step back to right horse as you chop block.

Grab the arm and kick the groin.

Step through and behind and strike throat with inside of thumb to forefinger.

Step under, lift arm over, and break the arm on your shoulder.

technique 98
Tangled Wings C

Defense for full nelson.

This is adequate, but there is a better defense. Simply drop down into a horse stance and punch to the front. That breaks the grip. Punch with the other hand if you wish. You are now to the side, so elbow to gut and poke the fingers over the shoulder to the eyes. This is out of Pinan (Heian) 3. I had opportunity to actually make it work, and it was so-o-o much easier than this one. That said, maybe this one will be easier for others. Have a bunch of people with different body shapes do this before making up your mind.

Step forward with one foot into bow stance as you punch down with the cross side arm.

Change feet, punching forward with the other arm and striking to the face with the elbow fromt he first punching hand.

technique 99
Siege of the Temple

Defense for two man attack. Front man right punches. Back man grabs right shoulder with the left hand.

Iconic Kenpo, with LOTS of problems.

First move is okay, and I can even work with the second move, but spinning the whole body to do a front kick on the third move? So-o-o many things could go wrong, even for the advanced student. It takes time, balance is at risk, and so on.

And, while you're spinning, what is the guy in front doing? A key across the ribs is not necessarily incapacitating, especially if the guy is wearing bulky or even loose clothing, or is just plain fat.

Then, while the guy in front is not completely handled, the hands get way too busy on the guy in the rear.

Step forward with the left foot into horse stance and execute a left inward block to the punch from the front and a right outward block to the grab from the rear.

Right raking key strike across ribs as you pivot 180 degrees on left foot and left chop to ribs of first attacker.

Right snap kick with simultaneous right Inward Block to rear opponent

Double chops to neck.

I can hear the arguments: you have to teach a guy to handle two people at once, and you have to start somewhere.

But not here.

This technique either needs massive overhaul, or to be tossed.

Vertical elbow to chin.
Claw to the face.
Cross out.

How about simultaneous block with a kick to the groin to the front. The guy in the rear is pulling, so let him pull, and help you align the turn of the body and the kick.

Then, starting your turn, you stick the guy in the throat with a spear and begin handling the guy in the rear.

Look, the basic problem with this technique is that you are splitting your intention. You don't fight two guys at the same time, you figure out how to fight one at a time, using them for sandwiches.

A sandwich is when you are the meat, and you keep both pieces of bread (the attackers) on the same side, and hopefully in the way of each other.

You shift to the side so that the guy coming from the rear is always trying to go around, but can't, until you are ready for him...which is to say when the guy in the front is dead bread.

There's a lot of problems here, as I said, and it stems from this basic problem of splitting intention, of being too clever and trying to fight two at once. I suggest taking a close look at passing techniques for the punch and creating a sandwich, which might entail getting together with an Aikidoist, and then trying to make his concepts into Kenpo concepts.

technique 100
Broken Honor B

Defense for a handshake.

Yikes! Another dreadful handshake attack! Quick, dispatch the villain for trying such a deadly maneuver on you!

Step forward and slap handshake up with left hand.

Left spike to ribs.

Grab the shake hand and swing down and up the other way.

Or maybe throw it out. Better ways to learn about breaking arms over shoulders.

Right elbow to rib cage.
Step through and circle under the arm.
Break the arm.

Funny thing, when I was researching this I didn't find it anywhere else. Could it be that the world doesn't believe a man can be attacked by a handshake?

A last thought, if you think the handshake is a set up, a chance to hold the hand immobile while a punch is launched with the other hand, then practice this one. It will actually work in that situation.

technique 101
Hooves of Death

Defense for a right punch to the face.

Hooves of Death. I think it was also called Dance of Death, taught to millions by the infamous Count Dante in his comic book course.

Step forward with the left foot and execute a left inward block. Right ridge hand to the groin.

Change feet as you grab the right knee with the left hand.

Step forward with the right foot and to the left with the right leg as you execute a right elbow into the stomach.

The set up for the takedown is wrong. Start the technique with the other foot forward and go right into it.

Hold the leg as they fall.

Back knuckle strike to the inside of the left knee.

Back knuckles to knees? The dance of Death just turned into the dance of irritation.

This is a figure eight motion, to a back knuckle strike to the inside of the right knee.

Right chop to the groin.

Grab the right foot and twist, turning the attacker over. The leg goes to the opposite side of your body.

Should have been done first, to protect yourself from a foot to the face.

Left knife edge kick to the floating ribs.
Left heel thrust to the kidneys.

Good practice for kicking, except that the knife edge isn't a good kick.

Jump over the body.

Land in a kneeling stance and execute a right chop to the back of the neck.

Right knife edge kick to the floating ribs.

Right Heel thrust to the spine.

Jump over the body.

Right knife edge kick to the head.

Cross out.

I don't know. I mean, it's iconic Kenpo, and there is an education in there, but...but it's so-o-o comic book.

Better to knock him down, turn him over, drop a knee on his back...simple and to the point, and workable.

Still, you almost have to teach it. Good or bad, comic book or not, you almost have to bow to the idea of it all.

technique 102
Approaching Night

Defense for a right punch from the side.

A little bit busy with the hands, but not bad. The funny thing is the only time I ever saw this block work it didn't have the first palm sliding up, it just worked with the second elbow raising up. Became quite devastating.

Cat stance away with a right windshield wiper block.

Left step behind with right claw to eye.
Left palm thrust to kidney.

Right back knuckle to back of head.

The above noted, I think I would take this technique to the first eye claw, then translate it into a throw of some sort. Maybe over the bow.

The thing is...when you have your fingers in some guys eyes, and he is reacting properly, and it's hard not to react in a set manner when somebody sticks their fingers in your eyes, one shouldn't back off from the technique, but rather go forward.

technique 103
Spinning Blades

Defense for a right punch with the left foot forward.

Lot of trouble with this one. Might be my notes, but like so m any techniques, the software has trouble with the distancing. Then the opponents end up too close, or out of position. The result is that I'm not sure whether I should have spun back for the kick (as I did), or spun all the way through.

Either way is weird, made more complex by the software's desire to be accurate, which tends to indicate that Kenpo is sometimes inaccurate.

Step forward with the left foot as you execute a left inward block.

Step across with the right foot and pivot, executing a right raking key strike to the ribs. (facing the open stance)

Finish spin with a left chop to the ribs.
Right kick to the groin.

Step forward and execute a ridge hand to the groin.

The point here is that whether it is my memory and notes, or the software or the distancing, there is a potential mish mash to this technique.

I like the spin to chop, except that you are turning your back to an opponent. Still, in the interests of strategy, and the fact that you are close and shouldn't increase the distance or do something weird, I would suggest spinning back with an elbow to the head. If you are going to use the foot you are close enough to use it for a sweep of some kind, but even that has weird potential.

And, just a note, some sources had this kick as a front kick, but that seemed to make the situation even more odd.

At any rate, taking all this into account, you should have a lot of fun if you try all the possibilities of this technique, if you wade through them looking for workability.

As is so often with Kenpo, it is not the techniques that are great, but rather the thinking that has to go into making things work, which, from that viewpoint, makes this a superior art. Now if you can make the techniques superior...

technique 104
Crossed Arrows

Two man defense. Man in back bear hugs with arms loose. Man in front punches with the right hand.

The block and kick are fine, if the guy behind you is not throwing you on the ground. Probably isn't, wants to hold you for the guy in front.

Right inward block with right snap kick to the groin.

Step right into horse stance and point arms up.
Bring elbows down on the forearms to break the grip.

But then the guy in front just...stays there! I know, he is supposed to crumple, so, okay. But do you really have all the time to break a grip and step behind somebody?

Step behind man two with the left foot in a horse stance as you execute an elbow spike to the sternum.

Right hammer to the groin.

Cross out.

A better technique would be placing your arm so his elbow is trapped, then simply turning. Guy flies through the air, or, at the very least, is set up for elbows to the center and the face.

technique 105
Wings of Iron A

Defense for a right punch to the face.

A little awkward, the hips don't align correctly with the hands.

Step forward with the left foot and execute a left inward block. Right elbow to the ribs.

Simultaneous left chop to the neck and right chop to the kidney.

After the glancing elbow you should strike with a knee, or spin (as in variation b on next page.)

technique 106
Wings of Iron B

Defense for a right punch to the face.

We're getting closer, but don't just spin back, spin and step and go for a grab art.

There is the fatal error here, of turning the back. Yes, sometimes it is necessary, but in this instance the solution would be to go for grab arts, which is the next closest distance when the distance in a fight collapses.

Step forward with the left foot and execute a left inward block.
Step through with the right foot as you execute a right elbow to the ribs.

Spin and elbow spike the ribs with the left arm.
Spin back and backfist the head.

technique 107
Crashing Waves

Defense for two hands to the throat.

I have always been curious about the over/under punch. I see it in other arts, it splits intention by having two punches, which can used, but as a last resort.

I have actually seen it used most efficiently as a method for picking up and carrying somebody, which makes it not defense, but a rescue technique. Hmmm. Maybe.

Step forward with one leg as you execute an over/under left punch to the face and right punch to the groin.

I have also seen it as a way to set up sweeping the grab away, as in the second step, and you have to wonder about ignoring somebody who's gripping your throat.

Still, I like it, you are out body parting (OBP) the two hands. Heck, if somebody is stupid enough to try choking you at arm's length from the front...almost anything will work, you know?

Step back, then sidestep to the side into a front stance as you execute an outward block.

Two finger gouge to the eyes.

So I would leave this in, but I would do the punuch to the ribs first, then the fingers to the eyes.

Pivot to horse as you execute a punch to the face.

Cross out.

I would be open to variations, however. I like throwing people on the ground rather than blinding them. More reality, more attention to control.

technique 108
Clawing Hawk

Defense for two hands to the throat.

I really like this. Short, sweet, compact, efficient, puts 'em to sleep.

Step forward shooting fingers to the eyes with both hands, overriding attacker's forearms.

Grab shoulder with left hand.

Pivot as you execute a right upward elbow strike.

My only problem is that I want more. Isn't it funny? Usually I'm saying' too busy,' or 'too much,' and now I am swinging the other way.

But this is the one that begs for a follow up claw to the eye, or, better, an inside foot sweep to a kneeling punch, etc.

Well, It is still sweet and one of the better Kenpo techniques. I'll probably put it a little earlier than blue belt, but we'll see.

About the Author

Al Case walked into his first martial arts school in 1967. During the Gold Age of Martial Arts he studied such arts as Aikido, Wing Chun, Ton Toi Northern Shaolin, Fut Ga Southern Shaolin, Weapons, Tai Chi Chuan, Pa Kua Chang, and others.

In 1981 he began writing for the martial arts magazines, including Inside Karate, Inside Kung Fu, Black Belt, Masters and Styles, and more.

In 1991 he was asked to write his own column in Inside Karate.

Beginning in 2001 he completed the basic studies of Matrixing, a logic approach to the Martial Arts he had been working on for over 30 years.

2011 he was heavily immersed in creating Neutronics, the science behind the science of Matrixing.

Currently he resides at Monkeyland, a location in Southern California where plans to build a martial arts temple are underway.

Interested martial artists can avail themselves of his research into Matrixing at MonsterMartialArts.com.

THE 'HOW TO CREATE KENPO KARATE' JOURNEY!

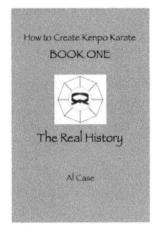  

The most incredible analysis of Kenpo Karate in the world.
In depth Matrixing of over 150 Kenpo techniques.
New ways of doing Kenpo forms.
New ways of teaching and structuring classes.
A COMPLETE REWORK OF ONE OF THE MOST
IMPORTANT MARTIAL ARTS SYSTEMS IN THE WORLD!

Over 40,000 words
Nearly 400 pages
Over 800 graphics

Only possible through…

the logic of Matrixing!

Pan Gai Noon (half hard/half soft) is a style of Chinese Kung Fu originally taught about 1900.

It was taught by a street hawker named Shu Shi Wa, and may have had roots in the Temple Gung Fu of the times.

It eventually was transformed into a style of Karate called Uechi Ryu.

The style therefore links Karate to Kung Fu, which makes it one of the more important martial arts, historically and technically speaking.

In this volume the art of Pan Gai Noon has been resurrected through the logic of Matrixing.

The first two forms, plus drills and techniques, are presented, making this a valuable addition to any martial artist's library.

Available on Amazon: Kindle or paperback

Kang Duk Won Korean Karate, the one Karate that resulted in the development of the five Korean systems which later became Taekwondo.

This is a pure form of Karate from before the Funakoshi and Japanese influence.

It was chosen by the Imperial bodyguards of three different nations, Okinawa, Korea, and Japan.

Available on Amazon: Kindle or paperback

Kwon Bup is a form of American Karate developed by Sensei Robert Babich of the Kang Duk Won. It is linear and powerful, and the ultimate expression of the only American to ever do the 'One Finger Trick.'

Sensei Babich could thrust a finger through a board and not break it, but leave a hole.

This is his art, his forms and techniques, his method of bringing Karate to the highest stage.

Available on Amazon: Kindle or paperback

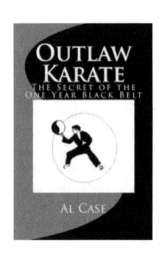

Outlaw Karate is the synthesis of two methods of Karate, Kang Duk Won (House for Espousing Virtue), and Kwon Bup (The Fist Method).

These arts were stripped of duplicate movements and poser techniques, then boiled down to six easy to learn (and thus easy to use) forms.

The result was a form of Karate that could be taught in less than one year, while keeping the original power of Karate, and even enhancing it.

This art set the stage for breakthroughs in the Martial Science of Matrixing.

Any karate student wishing to learn an extremely powerful form of Karate, and to delve into the history of Matrixing, should definitely look into Outlaw Karate.

Available on Amazon: Kindle or paperback

Matrixing is a form of logic.

While it can be used in any endeavor, it is specific to the Martial Arts.

Buddha Crane Karate is a very pivotal Martial Art as it was created just as the author was figuring out the logic of Matrixing.

In this book you get to see the exact thought process that is Matrixing at work; you will see the principles which would later crop up in his courses on Matrixing.

In addition, Buddha Crane is an entire Martial Art, built from the ground up.

Thus you get to see exactly, how and why an art takes form. This will definitely enlighten any who wish to inspect their own martial art and truly understand what they are seeing.

Available on Amazon: Kindle or paperback

The book that traces the evolution of internal power from Karate to Gung Fu.

There are three manuals in this volume, and they are designed to take the martial arts student from the hard knuckles of karate to the soft, internal practices of Gung Fu.

This book contains forms, techniques, training drills, and the theory necessary to help a student evolve quickly and natural.

Available on Amazon: Kindle or paperback

The Most Important Martial Arts Breakthrough in History

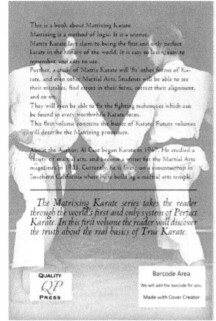

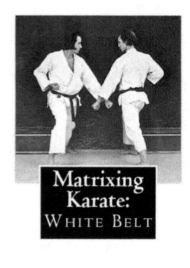

The Mysteries of the Martial Arts Resolved Through Matrixing

This is a book about Matrixing Karate.
Matrixing is a method of logic. It is a science.
Matrix Karate lays claim to being the first and only perfect Karate in the history of the world. It is easy to learn, easy to remember, and easy to use.
Further, a study of Matrix Karate will 'fix' other forms of Karate, and even other martial arts. Students will be able to see their mistakes, find errors in their forms, correct their alignment, and so on.
They will even be able to fix the fighting techniques which can be found in every worthwhile Karate form.
This fifth volume details the exact research used to discover the most significant breakthrough in Martial Arts history.

About the Author: Al Case began Karate in 1967. He studied a variety of martial arts and became a writer for the martial arts magazines in 1981. Currently, he is living on a mountaintop in southern California where he is building a martial arts temple.

The Matrixing Karate series takes the reader through the world's first and only system of Perfect Karate. In this last volume the reader will see the roots of Matrixing, and how it was actually developed.

QUALITY
QP
PRESS

Barcode Area

We will add the barcode for you.

Made with Cover Creator

Matrixing
Karate:
MASTER

AL CASE

MATRIXING KARATE
The Complete Series is available on Amazon.

There are companion DVDs to many of these books, and you can find them at:

MonsterMartialArts.com

Did you know...

Al Case has written over forty novels?
Many of them have martial arts sub themes.
Many of these novels are available on Amazon
either paperback or Kindle.
Or simply go to:

AlCaseBooks.com

CPSIA information can be obtained
at www.ICGtesting.com
Printed in the USA
BVHW04s1821230818
525444BV00009B/134/P